1997

COMMEMORATIVE
STAMP COLLECTION

UNITED STATES
POSTAL SERVICE

1997

COMMEMORATIVE STAMP COLLECTION

INTRODUCTION

This is the anniversary of many important American firsts celebrated on U.S. postage stamps. Nineteen ninety-seven is the golden anniversary of the U.S. Air Force and of the first aircraft to break the formidable sound barrier, the Bell X-1. I know, because I was there for both.

This book is filled with stamps that celebrate events that have not only shaped this great nation but also the world. Fifty years ago, the Marshall Plan helped Europe overcome the hunger and depression following World War II. The first U.S. postage stamps were sold 150 years ago. Even more amazingly, we have arrived at the 150 millionth anniversary of dinosaurs roaming Colorado, a time you'll see depicted on *The World of Dinosaurs* stamps.

The four covers of this unique book were taken from these stamps: *Humphrey Bogart, Classic Movie Monsters, Legendary Football Coaches,* and the wacky *Bugs Bunny.* By simply refolding and/or turning this book's dust jacket, you can display your favorite cover.

Other wonderful stamps included in this 1997 collection will excite young and old alike. You'll see stamps celebrating holidays like *Kwanzaa,* the *Lunar New Year* (Year of the Ox) and Christmas. Several stamps salute American opera singers as well as classical composers and conductors. Also included in this year's collection are: *Thornton Wilder,* author of the play, "Our Town"; *Helping Children Learn; Merian Botanical Prints;* two sheets of *Pacific 97; Classic American Aircraft; Classic American Dolls;* and the ever popular *Love* stamps featuring pairs of swans. On a more solemn note, a special stamp commemorates *Raoul Wallenberg* and his heroic efforts to save Hungarian Jews from Nazi death camps during World War II.

In 50 years, technology has advanced further than it did in the preceding 200. At the rate technology is changing the way we think and live, the pace as well as our thirst for knowledge accelerates more and more every day.

Chuck Yeager

Chuck Yeager

Brigadier General, USAF, Ret.

General Yeager has flown 201 types of military aircraft and has more than 14,000 flying hours, with more than 13,000 of these in fighter aircraft. He remains an active aviation enthusiast, acting as an **advisor for** various films, programs, and documentaries on aviation.

TABLE OF CONTENTS

THE WORLD OF DINOSAURS

28

The World of Dinosaurs
Grand Junction, CO
May 1, 1997

Carl Herrman
Art Director

James Gurney
Designer
Illustrator

John Boyd
Typographer

30.

Bugs Bunny
Burbank, CA
May 22, 1997

Terry McCaffrey
Art Director

Warner Bros.
Designer
Illustrator
Typographer

32

**Pacific 97
Re-engraved
1847 Franklin**
San Francisco, CA
May 29, 1997

**Pacific 97
Re-engraved
1847 Washington**
San Francisco, CA
May 30, 1997

Richard Sheaff
Art Director
Designer
Typographer

34

The Marshall Plan
Cambridge, MA
June 4, 1997

Richard Sheaff
Art Director
Designer
Illustrator

38

Legendary Football Coaches
The Pro Football
Hall of Fame
Canton, Ohio
July 25, 1997

Carl Herrman
Art Director
Designer

Daniel Moore
Illustrator

John Boyd
Typographer

36

Classic American Aircraft
Dayton, OH
July 19, 1997

Phil Jordan
Art Director
Designer
Typographer

William Phillips
Illustrator

40

Classic American Dolls
Anaheim, CA
July 29, 1997

Derry Noyes
Art Director

Sally Andersen-Bruce
Photographer

42

Humphrey Bogart
Los Angeles, CA
July 31, 1997

Carl Herrman
Art Director
Designer

Michael Deas
Illustrator

John Boyd
Typographer

46

Classical Composers & Conductors
New York, NY
September 10, 1997

Howard Paine
Art Director
Designer

Tom Mann
Typographer

Burt Silverman
Illustrator

44

Opera Singers
New York, NY
September 10, 1997

Howard Paine
Art Director

Mark English
Illustrator

48

Department of the Air Force
Washington, DC
September 18, 1997

Phil Jordan
Designer

Phillip Handelman
Photographer

50

Padre Félix Varela
Miami, FL
September 15, 1997

Carl Herrman
Art Director

Keith Birdsong
Illustrator

LUNAR
NEW YEAR

The family reunion dinner on **Lunar New Year** is a must for many Chinese households. Like all ethnic customs, some families follow traditions more closely than others. One tradition is shopping for **new shoes** since walking in old shoes on New Year's Day is supposed to bring bad luck.

Parades of revelers dance through the streets of Chinatowns throughout the United

States, celebrating the Lunar New Year, which this year—*Year of the Ox*—began on

February 7, 1997. On the final night of celebration, a paper dragon, the Chinese symbol

of goodness and strength, winds its way through the streets carried by men and boys

hidden under it. The noisy celebration wouldn't be complete without the loud popping of

strings of firecrackers. Festive meals and time to look forward to the coming year with hope

and anticipation also mark this holiday.

The *Year of the Ox* is the second year in the Chinese astrology calendar after the Year of the Rat. Because the ox drew the plow to help the Chinese with planting and harvesting, some feel it is immoral to kill and eat the ox. This belief probably entered Chinese culture through Buddhism. Because of the ox's association with plowing and planting, the ox also symbolizes spring.

This venerable animal wasn't always in such good favor with the populace. During the middle ages, emperors had to issue edicts banning the slaughtering of oxen by hungry citizens. In Japan, similar laws were enacted with harsh consequences for breaking them.

Folk tales recount many stories of oxen, often associating them with water and mystical occurrences. Because of their belief in the mystical power of the ox, at one time the Chinese threw stone or bronze figures of the animals into the rivers if the dikes were threatened.

This stamp, the fifth design in the Lunar New Year series, was designed by Clarence Lee, a Chinese-American who received design awards of excellence for his work on the first three stamps in the series.

Background: Paper dragon; opposite, inset: Acrobatics show at Spring festival in Beijing, China; top left: Drum players at Spring festival in Beijing, China; top right: Plum Blossoms by Chin Nung, Ching Dynasty; center: Lion dance at Spring festival in Beijing, China; bottom right: A pair of rampant dragons flanking a cusped projection in jade, 5th–4th centuries B.C.

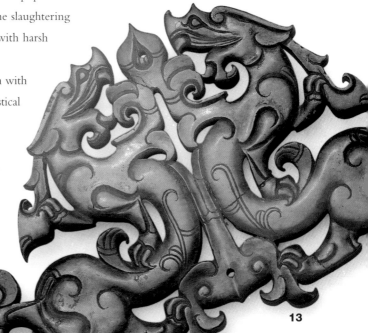

13

BENJAMIN O. DAVIS, SR.

In August, 1944, near the American front in France, an inspiring photo was taken of **Brigadier General Benjamin O. Davis, Sr.** on an inspection tour. **Designer Dick Sheaff** decided to use it on the stamp commemorating the general's career and **his contribution to the integration of America's wartime military.**

During World War II, Americans knew they had to pull together. The war's losses and suffering far overshadowed racial prejudice and bias in the country. Brigadier General Benjamin Oliver Davis, Sr. hoped the time was right for him to begin a racial healing process within the military. His accomplishments are commemorated on a new stamp.

Benjamin O. Davis was born in Washington D.C., where he spent his childhood. In 1898, he began his military career in the Spanish-American War and joined the regular army the following year. Two short years later, he passed the examination for a commission. He became the fourth person of color to attain the rank of officer in the U.S. Army.

With few opportunities to command troops, Davis rose slowly through the ranks. He became a colonel in 1930. During this period within his military career, he served as attaché to Liberia, was assigned to the Ohio and New York National Guards, and taught military science at Wilberforce University and Tuskegee Institute.

Davis's military career made history when, in 1940, President Franklin Roosevelt promoted him to brigadier general, making him the first man of color to become a general officer in the United States military. During World War II, he served with the inspector general in charge of a special section dealing with racial matters. Through this assignment, Davis traveled around the United States and Europe inspecting military camps, investigating racial disturbances, and working to improve the morale of black soldiers.

In 1944, Davis was able to convince the Army to try a limited type of integration. He received the Distinguished Service Medal in 1944 and the Bronze Star in 1945. Davis had three children, one of whom became a general in the United States Air Force.

Background and bottom left: Brigadier General Davis conducts close rifle inspection in England in 1942; opposite, inset: Group portrait of officers and executive committee of the NAACP in 1917. Davis is third from the left; center right: The Distinguished Service Medal and the Bronze Star.

LOVE

How do you describe love? It means many different things to different people; some even consider it indescribable. Love is alive and flourishing in the animal kingdom, as well. Like humans, many animals are monogamous and mate for life. They will often fight fiercely over a potential soul-mate and show feelings of deep remorse over the loss of a partner. It is only fitting that nature's role in love is recognized in this year's Love stamps picturing swans.

Swans symbolize serenity, beauty, and fidelity. Their gracefulness has inspired many works of art, poetry, music, and dance, including the popular ballet, *Swan Lake.* One study found that the most beloved animals to Americans are the dog, the horse, and third, the swan.

The male swan, called a *cob,* and the female, a *pen,* perform a unique courtship. They glide across still waters with a natural elegance, performing a courtship ritual that involves the intricate posturing of their heads. Once they've found their ideal partner, they remain together. Through their courtship and enduring relationships, these giant and regal birds have become the embodiment of eternal love.

This year's Love stamps are the 15th edition in the Love series. Love swans are the first stamps in this popular series that do not use the word "love." Instead, a heart, the universal symbol of love, is formed by a pair of swans, arching their necks to form a heart while gazing into each other's eyes.

For this year's Love stamps, artist Marvin Mattelson of Great Neck, New York, captured a beautiful and compelling image of two swans posed in the symbol of the heart.

Love is: two walrus lying together on rocks, a pair of orangutans embracing, two zebras in Zimbabwe, two King penguins, a couple of brown bears by a stream, and two lions cuddling.

Most **swans** mate for life. If one swan in a pair dies, the other mourns for a period of time. Some find other mates, but some never find a new mate, choosing to remain single.

HELPING CHILDREN LEARN

Today's **children** are immersed in the world of computers as fast as they can respond with a key-board to a monitor. It's never too early to help them **prepare for** the challenges of tomorrow with the technologies of today.

A little girl, about four or five years old, received a typical children's book about a kitten and its newly adopted human family. Sitting on her grandmother's lap, she opened the book, pointed to the first word in the first sentence, and read, "Kitty." She paused, continued with "has a new..." She paused again and then continued, "hoom... I mean home!" She stood, looked at her grandmother, and said, "I just read."

Place
Stamp
Here

BLACK BROWN VIOLET (PURPLE) BLUE GREEN YELLOW ORANGE RED

Teachers know that teaching does not drive the thirst for knowledge; discovery does. The *Helping Children Learn* stamp commemorates the nation's commitment to improve the education of all citizens.

President Clinton has announced a national literacy campaign called "America Reads," with a goal that every American child should possess the basic building block for learning—the ability to read—by the third grade.

The stamp issuance coincides with the 100th anniversary of the National Parent Teachers Association (PTA). This organization has been a bridge for families and educators to work together to improve the quality of education for students. Home-school communication is the fundamental goal of the PTA.

The National Education Association (NEA), founded in 1857, is a key driver of the process to provide quality education in the United States. The NEA was founded to advance the interests of teachers and to promote the cause of education in this country. Drawing its members from all walks of the teaching profession, the NEA is now more than 2.2 million strong and has invested more than 70 million dollars in public education improvements since 1983.

The Postal Service actively supports national goals to improve literacy through the "Wee Deliver" program. The in-school post offices provide a creative outlet and encourage students to develop reading and writing skills. Students compete to manage the school postal system where they collect, sort, and deliver "inter-school" mail to fellow students, teachers, and staff.

MERIAN BOTANICAL PRINTS

Most women of her time would never have considered it. Why would 52-year-old

Maria Sibylla Merian, with her youngest daughter in tow, set out on a two-month voyage to South America from

Amsterdam in 1699, a time when many women never ventured beyond the boundaries of their hometowns?

But Maria Sibylla Merian was no ordinary woman. She was born on April 2, 1647, in Frankfurt, Germany, the daughter of a Swiss engraver who died three years after her birth. Maria's mother then married a Flemish flower painter named Jacob Merell, who recognized Maria's artistic talent and helped her refine her skills.

Maria married Johann Andreas Graff, one of her father's students, in 1665. After moving to Nuremberg, she published a two volume book of flower engravings, *The New Book of Flowers*. The work closely resembled her father's style. She published three more volumes of her work with research and drawings on European moths, butterflies, and other insects.

Maria had two daughters, Johanna and Dorthea Maria. Both were trained in painting and engraving. After being introduced to a collection of South American butterflies, Maria's increasing interest led her on a two month voyage to Surinam to study the fascinating creatures of that far away land.

Each page of Maria's illustrations depicts plants and creatures in every stage of metamorphosis. This is a basic part of botanical and zoological illustration and is still used today. She was the first artist to illustrate the close link between various insects and plants.

Portrait and book at right from the original Merian book, "Der Rupsen Begin Voedzel," published in Amsterdam, 1683.

The art on these stamps is over 290 years old but looks as fresh as any painted today. Science and art have found perfect harmony through the talented and courageous **Maria Sibylla Merian.**

PACIFIC 97 STAGECOACH & SHIP

Imagine boarding a stagecoach for a journey that could take days, even weeks. In the mid-19th century, this was the only method of overland transportation available to travelers headed for the West. If the trip could be made by sea, they could book passage on a clipper ship, also a long and arduous journey.

Today, if we're in a hurry to get to our destination, we can take a plane. If we prefer, we can travel by bus, train, or automobile. If we're not in a hurry, boarding a modern-day cruise ship is an enjoyable, even romantic experience. While travel is still an adventure, we take it more for granted and usually look forward to it.

Paying tribute to those hardy pioneers who opened the West, two unique and first-ever triangular stamps have been created to commemorate methods of transportation representative of San Francisco 150 years ago. The first, an engraving of the clipper ship, Richard S. Ely, was inspired by a small advertising card handed out on the streets of eastern U.S. cities to encourage people to travel by ship to California. The second triangular stamp is a drawing of a U.S. Mail stagecoach, believed to be based on a drawing done by the artist-engraver, Harrison Eastman, who worked as a clerk in a San Francisco post office before he became known for his artwork.

The swaying of the coach and the listing of the ship give the viewer a glimpse into what was surely a sometimes perilous journey for the traveler of America's 1840s.

Place
Stamp
Here

Place
Stamp
Here

President Franklin D. Roosevelt

was just one of the famous men in

history who have been avid stamp

alike, have been, and are interested

in, the collection of rare stamps.

President Roosevelt is pictured

In 1939, **Thornton Wilder**
wrote a play, *The*
Merchant of Yonkers,
rewriting it in 1957 as
The Matchmaker.
Eventually, it became
the basis for the popular
musical, *Hello Dolly!.*
At the dedication of
this stamp, **Carol**
Channing sang "Hello
Dolly!" as a tribute to
the play and its author.

Place
Stamp
Here

THORNTON WILDER

How many of us have nervously stood on a high school stage ready to recite our character's lines from the play,

***Our Town*? As we played our parts without costumes, *Our Town* was literally our town. We learned how our**

characters interacted with others in the play, and the lessons we learned gave new meaning to the value of life.

As the only American author to receive three Pulitzer Prizes in fiction and drama, Thornton Wilder was no one-hit wonder. Born in Madison, Wisconsin, on April 17, 1897, he grew up seeing the world. His father, a member of the diplomatic service, took the family to Berkeley, California, Hong Kong, and later Shanghai. As a graduate of Yale, Wilder taught French at Cabala, a boys' boarding school, where he began writing his first novel, *The Cabala*. His next novel, *The Bridge of San Luis Rey,* was published in 1927 and became a runaway best-seller, selling over 250 thousand copies in a year and winning him his first Pulitzer Prize.

Wilder moved on to teach the Classics at the University of Chicago, where he also wrote more fiction. After completing his third novel, *The Woman of Andros,* in 1930, and his fourth, *Heaven's My Destination,* in 1935, he turned to writing for the stage. His first full-length Broadway play, *Our Town,* was produced in 1938. This instant American classic won him his second Pulitzer Prize.

Restless, Wilder spent a short time in Hollywood where he wrote the screenplay for Alfred Hitchcock's favorite film, *Shadow of a Doubt*. Yearning for the bright lights of Broadway, he returned to New York where he wrote the 1942 play, *The Skin of Our Teeth,* winning his third Pulitzer Prize. He returned to writing novels while continuing to write for the stage. Wilder worked at his home in Hamden, Connecticut until he passed away in 1975.

Opposite, inset: Thornton Wilder's Connecticut living room, ca.1935; top: First Lady, Mrs. Lyndon B. Johnson presents Wilder with the National Book Committee's National Medal for Literature; bottom right: Wilder in a scene from "The Skin of Our Teeth".

RAOUL WALLENBERG

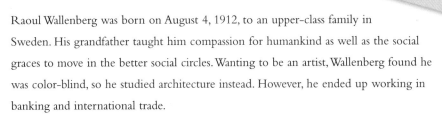

World War II, a war of epic proportions, was especially a nightmare for Jews. They could not imagine the hatred that had been unleashed on them. Families were torn apart; women, children, and the elderly were seized and interned in concentration camps. There was no place to hide from the German army, whose goal it was to find every Jewish citizen in any place that Nazi Germany controlled.

Raoul Wallenberg was born on August 4, 1912, to an upper-class family in Sweden. His grandfather taught him compassion for humankind as well as the social graces to move in the better social circles. Wanting to be an artist, Wallenberg found he was color-blind, so he studied architecture instead. However, he ended up working in banking and international trade.

In the summer of 1944, World War II was raging. The Swedish Foreign Ministry, with the approval of the Swedish branch of the World Jewish Congress and the United States War Refugee Board, decided to send Wallenberg to Budapest to stop the deportations of Hungarian Jews. He wasted no time issuing protective passes and other documents to stranded Jews. He also established safe houses in which Hungarian Jews could hide, and personally rescued Jews from vehicle convoys and trains.

In January 1945, he and his driver disappeared without a trace. According to Soviet documents, he died as a spy in a Moscow prison on July 17, 1947. Some theories suggest that he was spying for the U.S. More likely, he was recruited as an operative, not an agent, since he was not an American citizen.

Raoul Wallenberg is honored with his bust in the U.S. Capitol and in the U.S. Holocaust Memorial in Washington, D.C., where the stamp bearing his likeness was issued. In the words of U.S. Representative Tom Lantos, who was rescued by Wallenberg, "My wife and I owe our lives to Raoul Wallenberg—an authentic hero of the Holocaust."

Background: Jews gathered on the platform of the Josef Varos station in Budapest; center right: Letter of protection (Schutzpass), issued by the Swedish legislation in Budapest, to the Hungarian Jew, Lili Katz; center: The passport of Raoul Wallenberg returned in 1990 to Wallenberg's family in Sweden; bottom left: Monument to Raoul Wallenberg taken away by the Communist government the night before its unveiling in Szent Istvan Park and later re-erected in a pharmaceutical factory in Debrecen, without the inscription referring to Wallenberg; opposite, inset: Raoul Wallenberg in his Budapest office with his Jewish co-workers in November 1944.

"**Raoul** was never for a moment without thinking '**what can I do next?**' — he was like a machine," remembers **Agnes Adachi,** part of Wallenberg's rescue operation. "**Today's children** have to know what to fight for as Raoul Wallenberg did, because only the children without prejudice in their hands **can make peace in the world.**"

Place
Stamps
Here

THE WORLD OF DINOSAURS

Just the word "dinosaur" conjures up many images. We might see a huge monster lumbering through a dwarfed jungle. Or we think of the skeleton of an animal long extinct and never to be seen again. Some of us may be reminded of outdated machinery, as in "that computer is a dinosaur."

For most people fascinated by dinosaurs, it is the dinosaur as a living creature that is most exciting. From what scientists have determined, they lived from 225 million years ago until about 64.5 million years ago, becoming mysteriously extinct about 64 million years before humans. Thanks to the ingenuity and intelligence of humankind, people today can see and recognize creatures that inhabited the earth before they did.

The *World of Dinosaurs* stamps feature the prehistoric inhabitants from two areas of the United States. One is from the Jurassic Period of Colorado about 150 million years ago, and the other is from the Cretaceous Period in Montana about 75 million years ago. The dinosaurs in each scene represent the broad spectrum of life that existed in these ancient times. In the Jurassic scene, (carnivorous) meat-eating theropods and plant-eating sauropods, plant-eating Ornithischian dinosaurs, and flying pterosaurs, as well as a host of other creatures and plants from this era, bring the picture to life.

The Montana scene, during the Cretaceous Period, is very different from the earlier Jurassic Period. Many new plants and animals inhabited the area as well as the entire planet. Saurischian dinosaurs from the Jurassic period were few in number. In this scene, we see the meat-eating dinosaur, *Daspletosaurus,* and a bird-like running dinosaur called *Ornithomimus,* as well as the duck-billed hadrosaurs.

Background: Dinosaur footprints found in a quarry in Glenrose, TX, 1940; top: Charles Lang, Jeremiah Walsh, Charles Hoffman, and Paul Baltman working on Tyrannosaurus skull and jaws; center left: Sir Richard Owen was the man who coined the name dinosaurs meaning "terrible lizards"; center right: The flesh-eating dinosaur, "Ceratosaurus nasicornis"; inset: Barnum Brown and his assistants sorting "Hoplitosaurus" fragments.

A person must be deceased for at least 10 years to be eligible for an appearance on a **U.S. postage stamp.** Since the subject of these stamps, **dinosaurs,** have been extinct for **over 64 million years,** they definitely qualified.

B U G S   B U N N Y

Always grinning, Bugs Bunny would ask, "What's up, Doc?" With answers like "You — for dinner!," the inevitable chase began. Most of the time, the rabbit emerged much wiser and faster than any of his co-stars.

Bugs Bunny continues to be one of the most popular cartoon characters to ever grace a movie or television screen. The lovable, know-it-all rabbit looks as fresh as the day he made his debut on July 27, 1940, in the Merrie Melodies cartoon titled *A Wild Hare.* It was the beginning of a career that has spanned more than half a century and is still far from over. Bugs Bunny's first real contribution to his country came in 1942 when the patriotic rabbit encouraged Americans to buy war bonds. Dubbed a national hero and enshrined in the country's hearts for his war efforts, Bugs was awarded a service record by the United States Marine Corps and adopted as an official member of the Seabees.

In 1976, a market research study was conducted to determine the public's favorite personalities, both real and imaginary. Only Abe Lincoln tested higher than Bugs. Mayor Tom Bradley of Los Angeles declared December 21, 1985, "Bugs Bunny Day." The celebrations included the dedication of a Hollywood Boulevard Walk-of-Fame star for Bugs, making him the only other cartoon character besides Disney's Mickey Mouse to achieve this honor. From 1940 through 1964, Bugs was featured in nearly 200 seven-minute episodes and never took a single vacation.

A street-smart, tough, yet sometimes naive character, Bugs Bunny led an eclectic troupe of Warner Bros. characters, including Elmer Fudd, Daffy Duck, Porky Pig, The Road Runner, and Speedy Gonzales. Never underestimate the power of a smart aleck with heart.

DRAW EARS TO SUIT MOOD, WHISKERS TOO!

1½.

KEEP RUFF ON CHEEK HIGH IT MAKES HIM YOUNGER!

1.

2.

KEEP NECK FAIRLY SHORT!

LONG HANDS AND FINGERS!

3.

4.

WHITE OF E CONTINUES TO TAIL!

VITH POSE, PROPORTIONS DO NOT!

Place
Stamps
Here
LARGE FLAT FEET!

HAPE OF HEAD!

BUGS BUNNY
© L.S.P. ☆ 1943

BODY CAN STRETCH BUT RETAIN SAME VOLUME AS NORMAL POSES!

ARMS THICKEST AT WRIST!

LEG THICKEST AT ANKLE!

LOTS OF TEETH WHEN NECESSARY!

The Warner Bros. animators and directors were experts in making **Bugs Bunny** and his buddies look and act funny, but it took the voice of **Mel Blanc,** with what was once described as a "leather larynx," to complete the rabbit's personality.

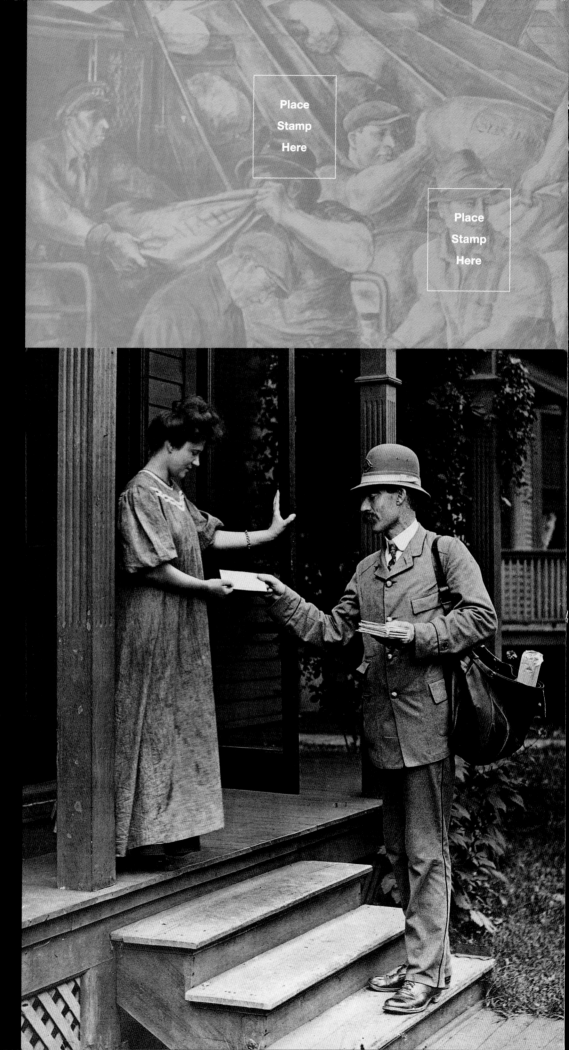

Place
Stamp
Here

Place
Stamp
Here

The parcel package room, in the **Van Buren Street post office in Chicago,** December 1929, was said to be the **world's busiest** for mail.

PACIFIC 97
FRANKLIN &
WASHINGTON

Paying a nickel or even a dime for a postage stamp would seem like a bargain today. But then we look at the price of a man's dress coat offered for sale in a newspaper in 1847—a mere five dollars. So you can see that, in 1847, a nickel or a dime was a lot of money—postage stamps were expensive.

At that time in the United States, the post office couldn't depend on motorized vehicles like planes, trains, or trucks. Sending a simple letter could take weeks and many pairs of hands helping to get it to its destination. Stagecoaches traveled through rugged country or clipper ships sailed through rough and often perilous seas carrying passengers, cargo, and random pieces of mail.

It was the Postmaster of New York who first suggested using stamps to the Postmaster General. They were originally engraved on steel plates by Rawdon, Wright, Hatch & Edson of New York City, a company known for its fine engraving of bank notes.

This year marks the 150th anniversary of the first U.S. postage stamps—the five-cent Benjamin Franklin and ten-cent George Washington. In honor of this anniversary, these two great American leaders are featured on reproductions of the original stamps in current denominations of 50 cents for the Franklin and 60 cents for the Washington. Each sheet contains an enlarged die proof of the original design and the wording "Pacific '97 San Francisco, CA from May 29 to June 8, 1997."

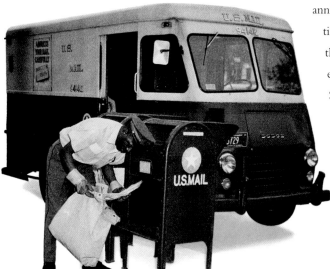

THE MARSHALL PLAN

In 1947, the United States knew it must become a leader in shoring up Europe's tattered economies and the dignity of its peoples. In shambles after the war, Europe needed a strong and daring plan. The war had destroyed more than cities and factories; it destroyed the hope of the people and paralyzed their economies.

With its politics in chaos, Europe had already swallowed five billion dollars in foreign aid from the United States. U.S. Secretary of State George C. Marshall realized that Europe's economic death could bring down the rest of the world so he decided a bold plan was needed to rebuild the continent, while leaving its people with dignity and an ongoing financial stability. He worked night and day to persuade American taxpayers and a wary Congress that investing additional billions was not throwing good money after bad. The investment would pay off, and the U.S. would be a stronger nation for it.

The plan was an ambitious one with three goals: to promote the participating countries' industrial, agricultural, and cultural production; to restore and maintain the strength of European currencies, budgets, and finances; and to stimulate trade within and outside the participating countries while reducing trade barriers.

By the end of 1947, polls showed that Americans understood the Marshall Plan and supported it. In March 1948, both the Senate and the House overwhelmingly approved the plan. Congress put strict limits on the amount of aid. The limits turned out to be unnecessary because, in two years, the benefits of the Marshall Plan were evident. One man's dream and conviction gave new life to a war-weary continent. In 1952, the Marshall Plan officially ended with a total U.S. contribution of just over 13.5 billion dollars.

·ALL OUR COLOURS TO THE MAST·

Top left: George C. Marshall with W. Henry Stimson, Secretary of War; center left: Nobel Peace Prize; center right: Poster honoring the Plan; background: Shipment of coal to the Netherlands for the European Recovery; opposite, inset: U.S. President Bill Clinton attends the Marshall Plan anniversary celebrations in Rotterdam.

Place
Stamp
Here

As part of the Dutch celebration of the 50th anniversary of **the Marshall Plan,** President and Mrs. Clinton joined some 4,000 guests for a party thrown by the city of **Rotterdam** honoring the United States.

FOR EUROPEAN RECOVERY

CLASSIC
AMERICAN
AIRCRAFT

From the bedroom ceiling of this average American pre-teenager hangs an amazing array of American aircraft.

Each is secured with clear nylon fishing line and looks to be in full flight. This model builder or mini-museum

curator probably knows more about each airplane than some seasoned pilots.

Classic American aircraft have always excited both young and old. The Smithsonian Air and Space Museum is like an extension of the bedroom full of hanging models. We can see the planes that made history by breaking world records or performing valiantly in enemy skies. The Smithsonian lets us see these magnificent machines up close, giving us the feeling we could have piloted one of these awesome aircraft.

Twenty aircraft have been chosen to be commemorated this year by the U.S. Postal Service. Each plane has provided some unique link in aviation history, leading to the sophisticated aircraft of today.

The first airplanes weren't fast and didn't fly great distances, but they were the forerunners of the fighters in World War I. The Wright B is the earliest plane featured as a stamp and was the next generation of improved airplanes seven years after the first flights of the Wright brothers. Next came the JN or Jenny that became the standard U.S. trainer in World War I. These planes were sturdy and after the war were used by barnstormers and in air shows.

During World War II, U.S. air power increased dramatically. New fighters were being developed as fast as they could be imagined. The bombers were further developed to carry incredibly heavy payloads with the fighters escorting them across enemy lines. The B-17 bomber was a workhorse, nicknamed the Flying Fortress. The Navy's Wildcat and Corsair made naval warfare history while the Army's Mustang and twin-engine Lightning were both fast and deadly.

These are just a few of the classic aircraft represented in this wonderful commemorative release. Enjoy all of the stamps in the series. Each airplane has its own unique place in history.

Bottom: Amelia Earhart, in 1932, became the first woman to fly solo across the Atlantic; background: The main cabin of the Boeing Stratocruiser, ca. 1948, gave passengers a chance to move around at will; opposite, inset: Wilbur and Orville Wright.

Place
Stamps
Here

Wilbur and **Orville Wright** started it all in December of 1903 with the first successful **manned** flight in a power-driven, heavier-than-air machine that covered fewer feet than the length of most of the passenger jets of today.

LEGENDARY FOOTBALL COACHES

One common denominator links successful football coaches: they're leaders first and winners second. On and off the field, they live what they teach — courage, hard work, strength — and their teams are living monuments to these traits.

Glenn "Pop" Warner (1871-1954) — In the tradition of winners, Warner was an innovative football strategist. He perfected the famous single- and double-wing formations, which are still used, as well as the naked reverse. He was the first coach to use the numbering system for plays and among the first coaches to use the huddle and spiral punt.

Warner's head coaching career lasted 44 years, during which he coached his teams to winning 319 games for Carlisle Indian School, Cornell, Georgia, Pittsburgh, Stanford, and Temple. In 1916 and 1918, he led national championship teams at Pittsburgh and in 1926 at Stanford. In the 1890s, he played football as a tackle for Cornell University. His classmates affectionately nicknamed him "Pop" because he was the oldest member of his freshman class.

Even today, Pop Warner's Little Scholars league for children provides a venue for young football players and cheerleaders. Many football greats have received their start in this program, and today the league is more than 250,000 strong in the U.S., Mexico, and Japan.

George Halas (1895-1983) — Holding the record for one man's association with a franchise in any professional sport, George Halas stayed with the Chicago Bears for 63 years as a player, coach, and owner. While playing in 1923, he set a record when he picked up an opponent's fumbled ball and ran it back for 98 yards.

As a head coach, he won an amazing 324 games during his 40-year career. He was the first to install a telephone on the sideline and the first professional football coach with a team fight song. His most notable coaching triumph was a 73-0 winning score against the Washington Redskins in 1940, a record still standing for the NFL championship game.

Before coming to Chicago, Halas played college football as an end for Illinois from 1915 to 1917. A talented all-around athlete, he moved from football to baseball, playing right field for the New York Yankees. Halas quit baseball after a stint in the minors because the Yankees had obtained a new right fielder, Babe Ruth.

Vince Lombardi (1913-1970) — In nine years, Vince Lombardi won five NFL championships with the Green Bay Packers, an incredible coaching feat.

His championships spanned the years 1961 through 1967, with Super Bowl wins in 1966 and 1967. Lombardi graduated with honors from Fordham where he also played football as a guard in 1935 and 1936, becoming a member of the famous line called the Seven Blocks of Granite. After college, thanks to his love for the game, Lombardi decided to go into coaching.

Lombardi's early years of coaching provided no clue of the success to come at Green Bay. He began as a high school coach, moved on to college assistant and then pro-assistant coach from 1939 until 1958. Today, Super Bowl winners receive the coveted Lombardi Trophy, created in memory of Vince.

Paul "Bear" Bryant (1913-1983) — Known as University of Alabama's famous "Bear," coach Bryant won a record 323 games, bringing home six national championships in 25 years. For 24 of those years, Bryant led his teams to bowl games. On the Alabama campus, his memory lives on through landmarks like Bryant Drive, Bryant-Denny Stadium, Bryant Hall, and the Bryant Museum.

Before Alabama, Bryant coached at Maryland, Kentucky, and Texas A&M, and before coaching, started out as a college football player for Alabama. As an Arkansas teenager, he wrestled a bear at a visiting circus, earning forever after the nickname "Bear."

Lombardi™ Estate of Vince Lombardi c/o CMG Worldwide, Indpl., IN

Vince Lombardi was an **expert at motivational speaking.** He once said, **"Football** is a great deal like life in that it **teaches** that **work, sacrifice, perseverance, competitive drive, selflessness, and respect for authority** is the price each and everyone of us must pay to **achieve any goal** that is worthwhile."

Place
Stamps
Here

Jules Verne, the famous French author, on a trans-Atlantic trip in 1867, wrote, "Among the passengers was a Frenchman who was carrying to America **30,000 papier-mâché dolls** which said the word **'Papa'** with a very successful accent."

CLASSIC AMERICAN DOLLS

They all have their own personalities and come alive in the hands of their owners. Anyone who has ever collected dolls knows that they are really just little people. It's not unusual to listen in on a child playing with a doll, talking to it, talking for it, and having it interact with other dolls.

The serious collectors know that there is more to their dolls than monetary worth. They are reminders of special events, cultural traditions, or the happy days of childhood. But the monetary worth can be staggering, depending on the condition of the doll and the fame of the craftsperson who created it.

Serious collectors are aware of the importance of accuracy. The clothing must be correct in every way. The costumes from other countries must be made from the actual fabrics produced there. The American-made dolls offer a glimpse into our national heritage as examples of different geographic regions and artistic styles.

Our collection of *Classic American Dolls* represents a wide range of doll-making throughout the history of our country. A variety of materials have been used, such as papier-mâché, cloth, wood, composition, hard plastic, and vinyl. Even though the materials used to make the dolls are cold and inanimate, through the skill of the creator, each of the dolls seems to take on a life of its own.

It's no wonder that each American doll maker featured on these stamps has woven a part of himself or herself into the doll. The colorful collection includes dolls named, "Alabama Baby", "Baby Coos", "The Columbian Doll", "Betsy McCall", "Raggedy Ann", "Skippy", "Babyland Rag", "Maggie Mix-up", "American Child", and "Scootles"; and examples by well-known doll designers and makers Martha Chase, Ludwig Greiner, Izannah Walker, and Albert Schoenhut; and a fine example of a hand-crafted Plains Indian doll.

Background: This is the happy smile of Debbie Kerrigan holding her mended doll, a product of Mrs. Hockaday's handiwork. Mrs. Hockaday spent 42 years mending broken dolls and little girl's hearts; center: A Martha Chase doll; bottom:The Schoenhut Circus.

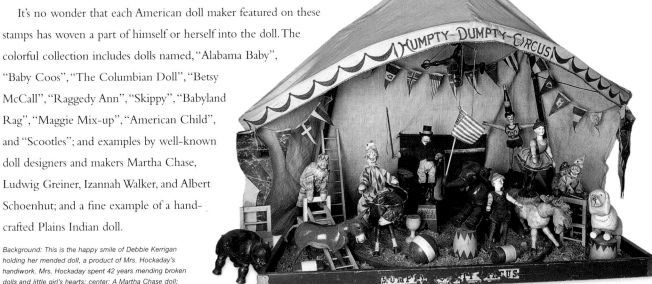

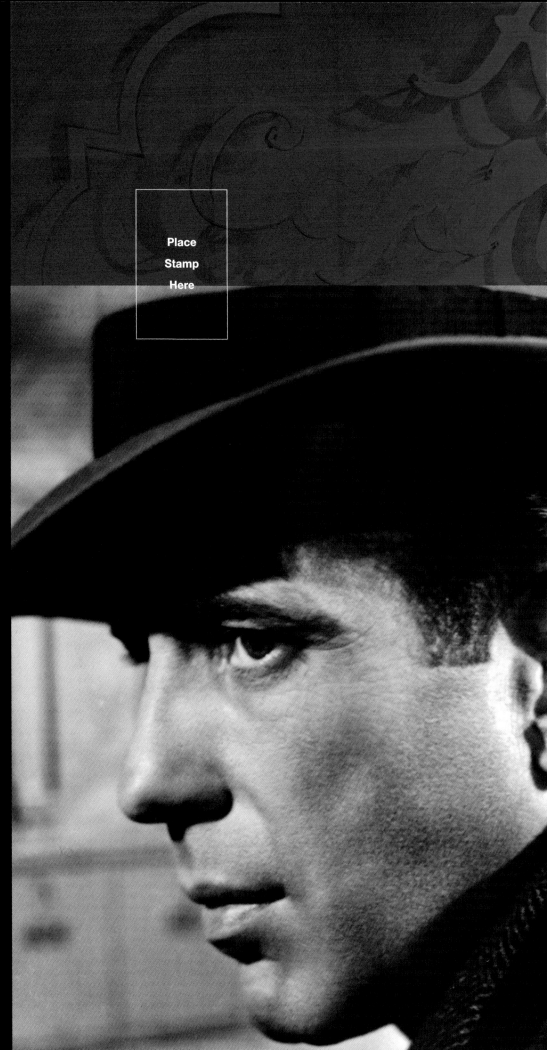

Place
Stamp
Here

"As Time Goes By" is the haunting theme song in **Casablanca,** one of the all-time great love stories set during World War II. Older than the movie, the song was **revived for the film** and rose to **incredible popularity** after Casablanca.

HUMPHREY BOGART

"Bogie," as he was affectionately known to all of his fans, personified the tough guy of the black-and-white film era. Well before his appearance in color movies, the drama of black-and-white film made Humphrey Bogart seem bigger than life. With a cigarette dangling from his mouth and a five-o'clock shadow, he usually played a world-weary cynic troubled by something in his past.

© A.M.P.A.S. ®

Whether playing an ex-con, war hero, detective, or a Riverboat captain in Africa, Bogart knew how to intrigue an audience. Through his anti-hero characters, his romantic appeal has spanned generations. Today, many people who have never seen a Bogart movie repeat lines from his films.

Born in 1899 to a prominent New York family, Humphrey DeForest Bogart began his career as an office boy before moving on to roles on the Great White Way of Broadway. He headed to Hollywood and the burgeoning sound film industry in the early 1930s. In 1930, he captured his third film role in *Up the River,* a prison film starring Spencer Tracy.

Bogart signed a contract with Warner Bros., known for tough guys like Edward G. Robinson and Jimmy Cagney. Bogie appeared in ten minor movie roles before his breakthrough performance in *The Petrified Forest* in 1936. Earning $550 a week, thanks to his featured player contract, Bogart now took off down the road to stardom.

Through the 1940s and 1950s, Humphrey Bogart continued to turn out cinema gems such as *The Maltese Falcon* in 1941, *Casablanca* in 1943, and his Oscar-winning *The African Queen* in 1951. In 1945, he married Lauren Bacall, and in 1947, he started his own film company, Santana Pictures. His last picture, *The Harder They Fall,* was released in 1956.

Opposite inset: Sam singing at Rick's Cafe; bottom: Claude Rains, Paul Henreid, Humphrey Bogart, and Ingrid Bergman in Casablanca (1942).

Bogart™ Bogart, Inc. c/o CMG Worldwide, Indpl., IN

OPERA
SINGERS

The cacophony of musical instruments rehearsing finally subsided. Moments later came a familiar tapping, slowly

replaced by the soft rich sounds of the orchestra in perfect harmony. The curtain of the New York Metropolitan

Opera House opened with a dazzling display of richly painted scenery and splendidly costumed singers.

When **Beverly Sills** was eight years old, she was taken to the Met to see her first opera *Lakmé,* featuring **Lily Pons.** Pons' costume was a daring two-piece outfit, exposing her bare midriff. Little Beverly loudly exclaimed to her mother and those surrounding them, **"Her belly button's showing!"**

When the "Met," as it was later nicknamed, first opened in October, 1883, it hosted European artists in popular European operas. During World War I, European singers couldn't make the crossing to America. One night in November, 1883, a young Connecticut-born **Rosa Ponselle** got her chance to make her debut opposite Enrico Caruso in Verdi's *La forza del destino.*

Ponselle's voice could be so powerful, yet so soft, that her talent to captivate an audience was said to have equaled Caruso's. She spent nearly two success-filled decades with the Met, setting vocal standards that are still unrivaled. After World War II, she returned from retirement to take the Baltimore Opera Company to new heights as its artistic director.

Another legendary singer, **Lawrence Tibbett,** began his meteoric climb to fame on January 2, 1925, at the Metropolitan, as the first American-born male artist to achieve stardom without European training. His performance as Ford in Verdi's *Falstaff* made him an instant star.

The versatility and range of his powerful baritone voice enabled him to sing opera in French, German, and Italian as well as music that was modern and popular at the time. While Tibbett's immense talent brought him fame and fortune, he still found time to organize the *American Guild of Musical Artists* for his fellow musicians, and serve as it's first president.

Barely five-foot tall, 98 pound **Lily Pons** made her debut at the Metropolitan Opera House on January 3, 1931, as the heroine of Donizetti's *Lucia di Lammermoor.* Her dazzling coloratura soprano voice reached notes that made her a star with her audiences and an inspiration to her contemporaries.

Her fame spread to Hollywood, then to radio, the recording industry, and finally, television. When World War II broke out, she unselfishly performed for Allied troops in European and Pacific battle zones.

In the 1930s and 1940s, America gave operatic talent back to the world on a grand scale. Amid the flood of newcomers was **Richard Tucker,** debuting in Ponchielli's *La gioconda* who sang at the Metropolitan Opera House for thirty years.

Born Rubin Tucker in Brooklyn, by age thirty, he became the best known cantor in the United States. He always longed to sing in Halévy's *La juive,* whose main character was a Jewish goldsmith, a part which had never been sung by a real Jewish cantor.

Almost 30 years later, he got his chance in a powerful European performance. Unfortunately, he never sang the part. He was struck down by a heart attack. His funeral was the first to ever be held at the Metropolitan Opera House.

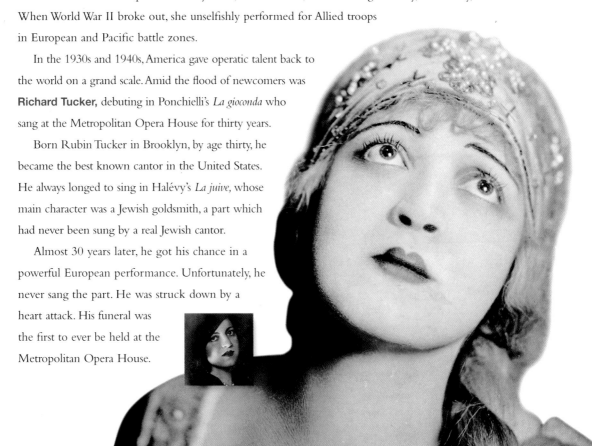

CLASSICAL COMPOSERS & CONDUCTORS

Composers never explain how they create. Not because it's a secret, but because the process isn't important, only the result. Leopold Stokowski (1882-1977) was described by Nicolas Slonimsky as a "celebrated, spectacularly endowed, and magically communicative English-American conductor." "Stokie," as he was called, conducted most music by heart.

Twelve years after Stokowski was born, another music icon made his way into the world. **Arthur Fiedler** (1894-1979), a tremendously popular American conductor, brought excitement to classical music, and his audiences loved it. Joining the Boston Pops, he became known as "Mr. Pops" and, later, was awarded the prestigious Medal of Freedom by President Gerald Ford.

Even in this era of musical greats, it was still a surprise when **George Szell** (1897-1970) made his debut as a pianist and a composer at age 11 and further astounded his peers by conducting an orchestra in Vienna at 16. Later, Szell found his way to Cleveland where his reputation flourished for nearly a quarter of a century.

Meanwhile, another youthful genius, **Eugene Ormandy** (1899-1985), was appointed Professor of Violin at the Budapest Royal Academy at the precocious age of 17. In 1936, Ormandy settled down in Philadelphia where he remained for 42 years. Studying voice in his youth, he was known as an incredibly strong orchestra builder, driving the Philadelphia Orchestra to new heights.

A celebrated composer, **Samuel Barber** (1910-1981), filled his music with the deep sensitivity of a melodist, which gave him the ability to handle intricate voice patterns. He was a master of orchestration, and his "Adagio for Strings" still receives many performances each year. The multi-talented Barber was also highly skilled at

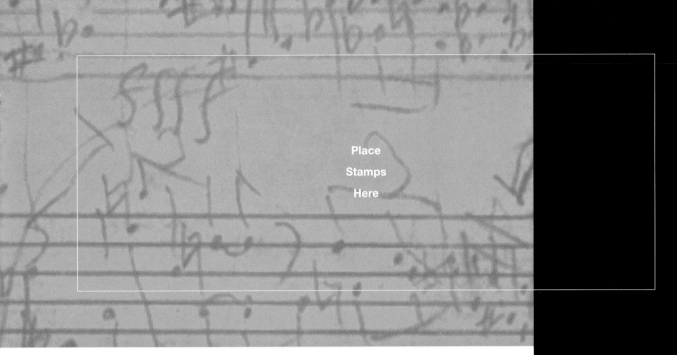

writing for solo instruments, so much so that instrumentalists seek out his work.

Growing up in New Jersey, **Ferde Grofé** (1892-1972), "Growfee" as he was called by his school chums, showed early signs of genius. He quickly became an accomplished composer, pianist, and arranger who excelled in every field he entered. Grofé joined Paul Whiteman's band in 1920 and arranged Gershwin's "Rhapsody in Blue" for its historic premiere performance, but he is best known for his own "Grand Canyon Suite."

Charles Ives (1874-1954) was "one of the most remarkable American composers, whose individual genius created music so original, so universal, and yet so deeply national in its sources of inspiration, that it profoundly changed the direction of American music," according to another great, Nicolas Slonimsky.

As the last composer in this series, **Louis Moreau Gottschalk** (1829-1869) was as much a popular concert pianist as he was a composer. In fact, he was called "the American Chopin." Unfortunately, after his death all but a few of his finest pieces were forgotten. One hundred years later, to the delight of music lovers everywhere, his work was rediscovered, and he took his place with the other greats of American music.

Background: Charles Ives' "The Unanswered Question"; opposite: Arthur Fiedler magically waves his baton; center: George Szell with Leon Fleisher; bottom: A candid look at Eugene Ormandy during a rehearsal; inset: Leopold Stokowski in a scene from "100 Men and a Girl".

**Leopold Stokowski —
"Stokie" — would star
before his audience
with his hands held up
high, motioning for
everyone to be quiet.
Then, with warmth and
compassion, he would
begin to explain the
subtleties of the music
they were going to hear**

DEPARTMENT OF THE AIR FORCE

"Off we go into the wild blue yonder" was the theme song that rang in pilots' ears during World War II. In khaki uniforms, the U.S. Army Air Corps was a new group of upstarts fast gaining respect from their ground troop brethren.

On April 1, 1954, Congress authorized the establishment of the **Air Force Academy.** Although it is considered a young upstart by the other military academies, the Air Force Academy is producing **top aviation talent and military leaders.**

Near the end of World War II, on its next-to-the-last scheduled
mission, the crew of the *Easy-Does-It,* an American B-17
bomber, flew out of Leipzig, Germany, toward its home base
in Bassingbourne, England. A glimmer of several enemy
aircraft on the horizon caught the pilot's eye. German
fighters approached the big "Flying Fortress" at an
incredible speed. Motioning to his co-pilot, the
pilot pointed toward the German aircraft.
Something wasn't right—there were no pro-
pellers on these airplanes. Suddenly, without warn-
ing, the fighters climbed straight up—a feat no American plane could duplicate.

It didn't take the U.S. Government and the military long to realize that wars
were going to be fought in the air and that air power was going to be crucial to
the nation's defense. The U.S. Army Air Corps became the United States Air
Force in 1947. Fifty years later, this branch of the service has participated
in conflicts all over the globe and has been instrumental in winning them.
The Air Force is an important part of the military's tactical warfare, offer-
ing its support to the Army, Navy, and Marine Corps, and being involved
in skirmishes on both land and sea.

The Department of the Air Force, like the other branches of the
service, has its own civilian secretary, currently Dr. Sheila E.
Widnall, who heads up the department under the secretary
of defense. The secretary of the Air Force ranks equally with
the secretaries of the Army and Navy.

No longer is it "Off we go into the wild blue yonder."
The Air Force is deeply involved in space technology
and exploration as well as the role it will play in the
twenty-first century. Maybe the Air Force's anthem should
be rewritten "Off we go into the starry black yonder."

Background: Whirling Device; opposite inset: USAFA, Colorado; top: Secretary of the Navy John L.
Sullivan and the nation's first secretary of the Air Force, Stuart Symington, took office as the armed forces
unification act became effective; center right: The "jet age" showed the importance of air power; bottom: F-86
Sabre jet pilot, First Lt. Joseph McConnell, Jr. of Apple Valley, California, became the 27th jet ace of the Korean War.

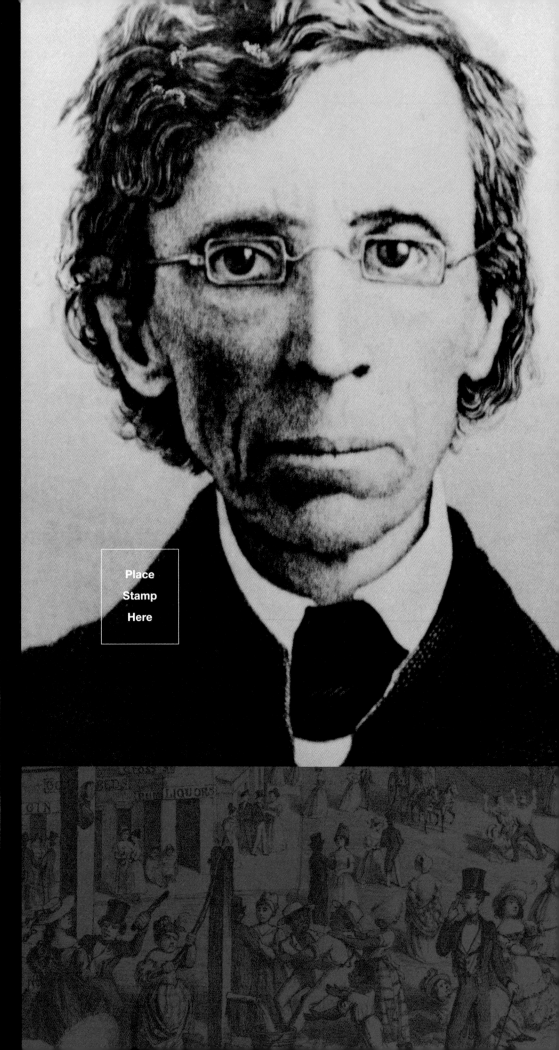

Padre Varela founded the **Church of the Transfiguration** which still exists today and is often called the **Church of the Immigrants.** The parish has evolved from one of Irish immigrants to Italian immigrants and is now almost 100% Chinese.

Place
Stamp
Here

PADRE FÉLIX VARELA

The cries of the sick and dying echoed through the halls of the small New York City hospital. The year was 1832, and the cholera epidemic was in its most destructive stages. Padre Félix Varela made his way from patient to patient and hospital to hospital, virtually living with the victims of the disease.

Padre Varela had always dedicated his life to the sick and poor minorities of New York City with special attention to the Irish immigrants' young and helpless. Before the epidemic, he founded nurseries and orphanages for the children of poor widows. He also organized the New York Catholic Temperance Association. As a tribute to his dedication, he was named Vicar General of New York City.

Padre Varela did not stop with ministering to the poor and sick, he also founded the first Spanish-language journals in the U.S., publishing articles and essays about human rights' injustices suffered by minorities. In addition, he published religious essays on tolerance and cooperation between English and Spanish speaking communities in the city.

Born in Cuba in 1788, Varela became a Professor of Philosophy at the Seminary of San Carlos in Havana where he was known and admired as a great educator. His role in providing women with the same educational opportunities as men was controversial at the time but gave women chances they otherwise wouldn't have had.

Because of illness, Varela retired from his humanitarian duties and spent his last years in the city of St. Augustine, Florida, where he died in 1853.

Opposite inset: Parish records from the Chuch of the Transfiguration with Félix Varela's signature; background: "Five Points", 1827, largely immigrant area of lower Manhatten where Padre Varela worked; center: New York Hospital, ca.1830; center left: Cholera Broadside listing remedies, 1832; center right: "The Catholic Expositor", a monthly periodical edited by Félix Varela; bottom: Church of the Transfiguration, late 19th century, after relocation to present site. The original Parish was founded by Padre Varela in 1827.

C L A S S I C

M O V I E

M O N S T E R S

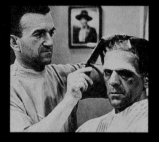

The creation of
Frankenstein, the
classic movie monster,
was an ordeal for both
the famous make-up
artist, **Jack Pierce,** and
Boris Karloff, the actor
who played the role.
The process began at
5:30 every morning
and took 3-1/2 hours
to complete.

WARNING!! If you have a weak heart and cannot stand excitement, we advise
you not to see *Dracula.* However, if your nerves can stand electrifying drama,
then we dare you to see *Dracula.* This is how the ad read in 1931.

Immortalized in Universal Studios, these famous ghoulish characters are a
legacy in a genre that continues to attract movie fans today. Like any fine
work, the films of these famous monsters are considered "classics" in the
truest sense. While the films lack the computerized special
effects now used, the actors and their monsters
were as convincing to their audiences as
any creature created today.

The Phantom of the Opera. Deep in the catacombs beneath Paris, "the man of a thousand faces," Lon Chaney, Sr., plays the organ as the film's heroine removes his mask. The audience watches the silent drama in awe. Suddenly, everyone shrieks in terror at the disfigured face of the man beneath the mask. In 1925, Lon Chaney and Universal Studios made the monster live for thousands of viewers.

Dracula. It's hard to say the name without using the thick European accent attributed to the count himself. Bela Lugosi, the Hungarian actor who immortalized the 500-year-old vampire, came to America in the 1920s and performed Bram Stoker's character, Dracula, on stage over a thousand times. In the 1931 Universal Studios' film Bela Lugosi brought his famous character to movie screens across the nation, hypnotizing audiences with his accent and promise of eternal life in death.

Frankenstein. Young Mary Shelley wrote the book about an obsessed doctor who created a monster from the body parts of corpses. Appearing on the screen in 1931, the Universal Studios' film was an instant hit. A relatively unknown actor named Boris Karloff made national acclaim in the film and mesmerized audiences with his portrayal of the monster. Just as Bela Lugosi made himself into Dracula, Boris Karloff became Frankenstein's monster. Though he frightened movie goers with his monster antics, Karloff was, in reality, a mild-mannered English gentleman who continued to act until his 80th year.

The Mummy. A 3700-year-old mummy returns to life to terrorize film goers. According to Egyptian legend, the High Priest, Imhotep, buried in the ancient sands of Egypt, has been waiting for the Scroll of Troth to give it new life. In 1932, just one year after portraying Dr. Frankenstein's monster, Boris Karloff brought Imhotep to the screen and found a new character through which to scare the wits out of "hungry-for-horror" movie audiences.

The Wolf Man. The screenplay of the werewolf, half man and half wolf, was created by Curt Siodmak, who today is 93 years old. Had Lon Chaney, Sr. not died tragically in 1930, the part of the werewolf in the movie version would have been perfect for him. Instead, Chaney's son, Creighton, known as Lon Chaney, "Jr.", played the part of Lawrence Talbot, the ill-fated man who became half wolf after the wolfbane bloomed. In 1941, caught in the midst of a real and terrible war, audiences who saw the Universal Studios' movie got a chance to conquer the imaginary monster and their fears by just leaving the theater. Lon Chaney, Jr. would portray a werewolf seven times before the end of his career.

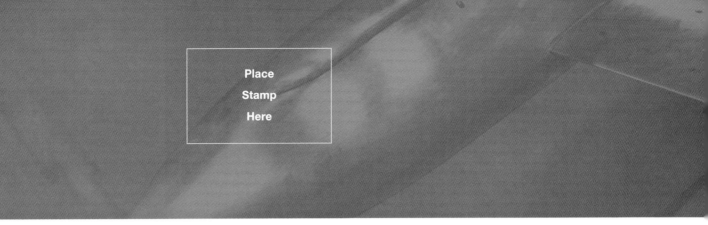

FIRST SUPERSONIC FLIGHT

They said it couldn't be done. It would crash, blow up, or disintegrate. Imagine, a plane flying as fast as the speed of sound. Besides, man wasn't supposed to fly in the first place.

Scientists knew that small objects, such as bullets and artillery rounds, could travel faster than the speed of sound. Even massive rockets, such as the German V-2s flew faster than the speed of sound, but the rockets were just big bullets. But an airplane was different. It took a huge amount of fuel to reach high speeds, and the higher the speed, the more fuel was needed. The stresses on the wings and the plane's body would be awesome. For scientists of the 1940s, the challenge of combining enough power with a sturdy structure capable of withstanding the shock waves seemed impossible.

At the end of World War II, the U.S. National Advisory Committee for Aeronautics, working separately with the Navy and Air Force, began working on different approaches to attaining high-speed flight. Bell Aircraft Corporation, using engines by Aerojet Engineering Corporation, won the contract to build three X-1 aircraft. The X-1 was no normal airplane; it was a rocket, fueled with liquid oxygen and alcohol propellants and driven by a 6,000-pound-thrust engine. To conserve fuel, the X-1 would be carried aloft by a specially fitted B-29 bomber and released.

Being the first country to break the sound barrier was a matter of national prestige, but the military implications were considered much more important. Because of the sensitive nature of the program, there were few press releases or open acknowledgment of the program to the general public.

The ninth test flight of the X-1 was a routine mission. The B-29 "mother ship" flew east of what is now Edwards Air Force Base, California, turned west, and dropped the X-1 at an altitude of 20,000 feet. Test pilot Captain Charles E. (Chuck) Yeager ignited all four rocket chambers and climbed. To avoid overshooting the assigned altitude of 40,000 feet, he shut down two chambers. After leveling off, he lit the third chamber, and the rest is history. On October 14, 1947, Captain Yeager became the first pilot to break the sound barrier.

After the flight, tests continued, but the achievement remained a military secret until June, 1948. Chuck Yeager received the prestigious Mackay Trophy for 1947's most meritorious flight by a member of the Air Force.

Six years after his historic flight, **Yeager** set another speed record on December 12, 1953, by flying two and one half times the speed of sound in a Bell X-1A. After his record-breaking career as a test pilot, he went on to become commandant of the Aerospace Research Pilot School at Edwards Air Force Base in California.

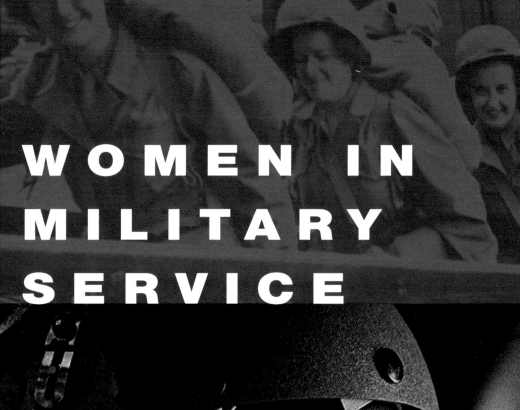

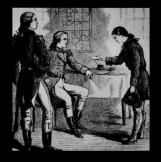

WOMEN IN MILITARY SERVICE

Women of the American

Armed Services are

honored on this colorful

stamp. Each of the ser-

vices is represented by

a woman wearing the

uniform of her branch.

The stamp celebrates

the ever changing role

of women in positions

of leadership within the

armed services.

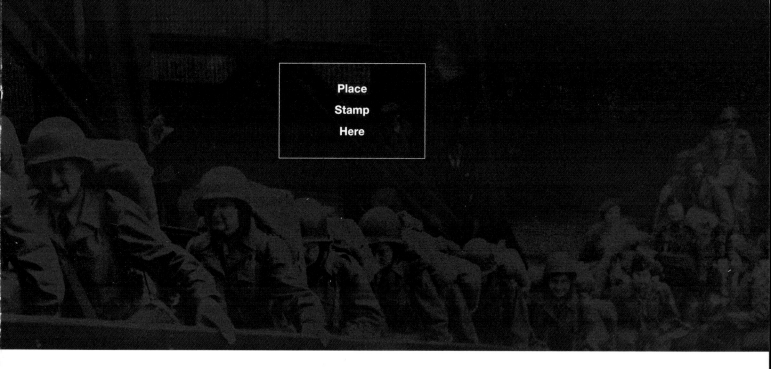

The acrid smoke-filled air hung over the battlefield of Antietam. It was September of 1862. The war was the costliest of all of the wars the U.S. would participate in to date. It was the Civil War with American against American and nurses on both sides performing the heroic tasks of caring for the tired and bleeding.

Although there were fewer casualties during World War I, women volunteered for service by the thousands. American women have served their country as nurses, spies, soldiers, or wartime journalists. They have shown their bravery over and over again behind the front lines as well as on them.

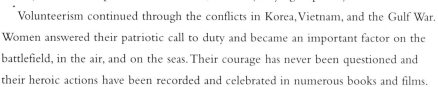

World War II saw women for the first time, openly recruited to support and free-up men for combat positions. This was the birth of the women's branches of the armed services. The branches include: the WACs (Army); WAFs (Air Force); WAVEs (Navy); SPAR (Coast Guard); Marine Corps Women's Reserve; WASPs (ferrying airplanes).

Volunteerism continued through the conflicts in Korea, Vietnam, and the Gulf War. Women answered their patriotic call to duty and became an important factor on the battlefield, in the air, and on the seas. Their courage has never been questioned and their heroic actions have been recorded and celebrated in numerous books and films.

The Gulf War of 1991 was the latest proving ground for women under fire. Again they performed difficult tasks, and were a credit to the uniforms they wore. With tech-

nology increasing, brain not brawn, has become the key to successful battlefield operations. Physical stamina is still needed, but not confined to either gender.

Today, as the frontier of space continues to grow, women are taking on new roles in command of sophisticated air and space craft. The women of previous wars would be proud to see the limitless future for women in military service today.

Background: England, 1944, a group of U.S. Army WACs board a troop transport on their way to France; opposite inset: Deborah Samson presenting a letter to Gen. Washington; center: A Navy pilot stands ready for duty; bottom: Women in the Marines.

HOLIDAY TRADITIONS & CELEBRATIONS

Holidays are a time for peace, understanding, and harmony. We also remember those who gave society something positive. Our holiday symbols can be human likenesses or elements of nature that remind us of the significance of the occasion. This year, through stamps, we look at images that have special meanings for Americans.

The traditional Madonna and Child (Virgin Mary and infant Jesus) holiday stamp is based on Christian beliefs that have inspired many works of art. The Madonna and Child are among the most important and familiar art subjects taken from Christianity.

The image on this year's stamp is the classic Madonna and Child with Saints and Angels (circa 1471), a detail of a painted wood panel in the National Gallery of Art, Washington, DC, by artist Sano di Pietro (1406-1481). The partially visible inscription on the halo reads "ave gratia plena do (minus tecum)," which means, "Hail, full of grace, the Lord is with thee," a phrase taken from the Bible (Luke 1:28).

The sprig of American holly is another traditional holiday symbol. The rich green leaves and vivid red berries give it a natural elegance. Conjuring up thoughts of snow, a warm fire, and savory home-cooked foods, the holly on our holiday stamp reminds us of a season of love, the giving of gifts, and the laughter of children. The American holly on this stamp is the work of the talented artist, Ned Seidler, known for his botanical illustrations.

The celebration of Kwanzaa inspired one of our most colorful stamps. Introduced in 1966, Kwanzaa, a cultural festival that takes place from December 26 to January 1, is a time for peace and unity within the African-American community.

Intended to be a harvest celebration, Kwanzaa stretches over seven days, each one dedicated to one of the seven principles called Nguzo Saba. Unity, Self-determination, Collective work and responsibility, Cooperative economics, Purpose, Creativity, and Faith are the seven principles. They are meant to ensure a good life in peace with your neighbors.

Kwanzaa has become a cultural festival celebrated by millions of people in the United States, Canada, the Caribbean, and England. Although Kwanzaa was created in the U.S., it is even celebrated in Africa.

The festive art featured on the Kwanzaa stamps is the work of Synthia Saint James, a self-taught artist. Her speciality is Kwanzaa-related theme art with its vivid colors and bold shapes.

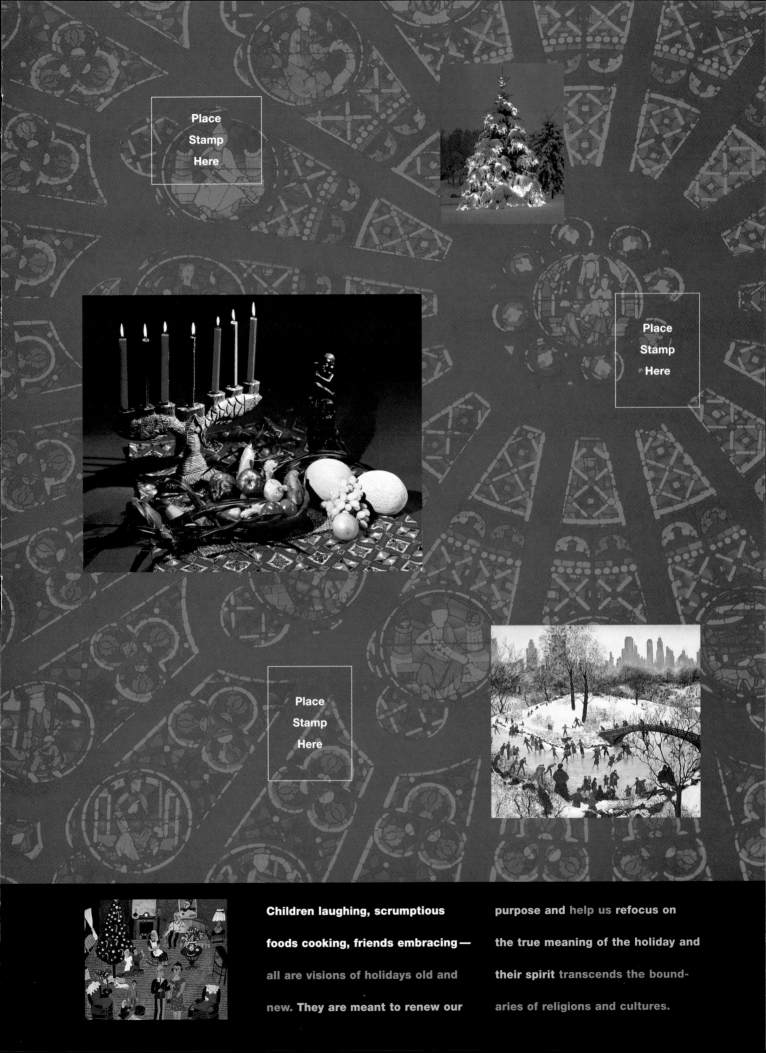

Place
Stamp
Here

Place
Stamp
Here

Place
Stamp
Here

Children laughing, scrumptious foods cooking, friends embracing— all are visions of holidays old and new. They are meant to renew our purpose and help us refocus on the true meaning of the holiday and their spirit transcends the boundaries of religions and cultures.

PHOTO
CREDITS

Raoul Wallenberg

Page 26

(background) Thomas Veres, courtesy of USHMM Photo Archives

(right below) Lena Kurtz Deutsch, courtesy of USHMM Photo Archives

(right above) Courtesy of USHMM Photo Archives

(bottom left) Thomas Veres, courtesy of USHMM Photo Archives

Page 27

Courtesy of USHMM Photo Archives

(inset) Thomas Veres, courtesy of USHMM Photo Archives

The World of Dinosaurs

Page 28

(background) R.T. Bird, photographer. Courtesy of Dept. of Library Services, American Museum of Natural History, #132132

Page 29

(clockwise from top right)

Courtesy of Dept. of Library Services, American Museum of Natural History, #129039

Smithsonian Institution, National Museum of Natural History

H. S. Rice, photographer/ Courtesy of Department of Library Services, American Museum of Natural History, #314221

Library of Congress, #LC-USZ62-11244

Bugs Bunny

Page 30

(clockwise from top left)

Courtesy of Joe Adamson

Courtesy of J. Michael Barrier

USPS

Page 31

(background) Courtesy of J. Michael Barrier

Courtesy of J. Michael Barrier and Joe Adamson

(inset) Warner Bros. Archives, University of Southern California

Pacific 97

1847 Franklin / Washington

Page 32

(inset) Library of Congress, #LC-USZ62-115167

(background) USPS: *Post Office Interior,* mural by Reginald Marsh

USPS

Page 33

USPS

The Marshall Plan

Page 34

(top left) Archive Photos

(all others) Courtesy of The George C. Marshall Foundation

Page 35

(portrait) Library of Congress

(inset) AP/Wide World/Scott Applewhite, photographer

Classic American Aircraft

Page 36

(top) Archive Photos

(middle) UPI/Corbis-Bettmann

(bottom) Corbis-Bettmann

Page 37

(background) National Archives

AP/Wide World

Legendary Football Coaches

Page 38

(all) UPI/Corbis-Bettmann

Page 39

(clockwise)

AP/Wide World

UPI/Corbis-Bettmann

UPI/Corbis-Bettmann

(inset) AP/Wide World

AP/Wide World

AP/Wide World

Classic American Dolls

Page 40

(background) Archive Photos Corbis-Bettmann

Page 41

(all) Courtesy of The Washington Dolls' House and Toy Museum

Humphrey Bogart

Page 42

(background) The Kobal Collection

(portrait) The Kobal Collection

(inset) Wisconsin Center for Film and Theatre Research

Page 43
(clockwise from top right)
Wisconsin Center for Film
and Theatre Research
The Kobal Collection
The Kobal Collection
(Oscar) Academy of Motion
Picture Arts and Sciences
Wisconsin Center for Film
and Theatre Research

Opera Singers
Page 44 & 45
(all) Courtesy of
Metropolitan Opera Archives

Classic Composers &
Conductors
Page 46
(background)
Charles Ives Papers,
Yale University Music Library
©1953 Peer International Corp.
Reprinted by permission
Archive Photos
Page 47
(all) Archive Photos

Department of the Air Force
Page 48
(background) National Archives
Courtesy U.S. Air Force Academy
Page 49
(clockwise from top)
UPI/Corbis-Bettman
National Archives
AP/Wide World

Padre Félix Varela
Page 50
(left) Church of the
Transfiguration
(portrait) Félix Varela
Foundation, New York
(background) Museum of the
City of New York
Page 51
(top left-broadside)
Collection of the New York
Historical Society
Museum of the
City of New York
(middle) Library of Congress
(bottom) The Church of the
Transfiguration and Archdiocese
of New York Archives

The Classic Movie Monsters
Page 52
The Kobal Collection
Page 53
(top left) Photodisc
(top right) Archive Photos
(all others) The Kobal Collection

First Supersonic Flight
Page 54
(background) National
Aeronautics and Space
Administration, Langley
(portrait) Courtesy of Air Force
Flight Test Center, History
Office, Edwards AFB
Page 55
Courtesy of Air Force Flight
Test Center, History Office,
Edwards AFB
(inset) ©1947, Los Angeles Times.
Reprinted by permission.
(bottom) National Aeronautics
and Space Administration,
Dryden Research Center

Women In Military Service
Page 56
(background and inset)
UPI/Corbis-Bettman
DVIC Motion Media
Records Center
Page 57
DVIC Motion Media
Records Center

Holiday Traditions &
Celebrations
Page 58
Katsuyoshi Tanaka,
photographer/Woodfin Camp
Harold Dorwin, photographer/
Smithsonian Folklife Studies
Page 59
(top to bottom) ComStock
Harold Dorwin, photographer/
Anacostia Museum
©National Museum of American
Art, Washington DC/ Art
Resource, NY
©Malcah Zeldis,
Art Resource, NY
(background) ComStock

Photo Credits
Page 60
Corbis-Bettmann

Page 61
(top to bottom)
Library of Congress,
Rare Book Division
©1997 Christopher Liu/
ChinaStock
Illustration courtesy of
K. Bopp
National Museum of American
Art, Washington, DC/
Art Resource, NY
Page 62
Archive Photos
USPS

Page 63
The Kobal Collection
Archive Photos
Page 64
UPI/Corbis-Bettmann

Acknowledgements
Special thanks to the following
individuals for their contribu-
tions to the production of
this book.
The stamps and this book were
produced by Stamp Services,
United States Postal Service.

United States Postal Service
Marvin Runyon
Postmaster General and
Chief Executive Officer
Allen Kane
Chief Marketing Officer
Azeezaly S. Jaffer
Manager, Stamp Services
Wanda Parks
Contract Administration
Paul Ovchinnikoff
Print Supervision
Manuel P. Vasquez
Project Management

Sparkman + Associates, Inc.
Don Sparkman
Copywriting and editing
Christopher J. Paul
Art direction and design
Robert McVearry
Associate design and production
Siewwah Teo
Production assistance

Corinne Szabo
Picture Research
Visual and historical research

Waring Photography, Inc.
Three dimensional and
studio photography

Sherri Alms
Editorial assistance

PhotoAssist, Inc.
Fact verification

If you can read this,
this book is upside down.
Flip it over and read it from
the other end.